— CHILD INTERWOVEN —

MEMORIES
IN POEM AND PROSE
of
A RUSSIAN GIRLHOOD IN 1940S SHANGHAI

— *Marina Romani* —

Park Place Publications
www.parkplacepublications.com

Acknowledgments

My thanks to the journals *Homestead Review* and *Porter Gulch Review*, which originally published earlier versions of the following poems: "Baba Yaga," "Cicada Summer," "Interwoven," "My Grandmother Vera Kirill'na," and "Summer Train Ride."

All photos are from my personal collection, with the following exceptions: views of a Chinese city, in the frontispiece collage background, appeared on the Internet—the source was not identified; images of me as an adult, on page 71 and on the back cover, are my adaptations of color photographs by Elena Taurke and Nikolai Loveikis respectively.

In matters of cover text, I thank Alice Tao for the Chinese title of this book and the gift of my Chinese name; I have greatly benefitted from discussions with Olga Matich and Ludmilla Elinson about possible, and impossible, variants for a Russian title, but the version that appears is of my own making.

Cover, frontispiece, and book design by Marina Romani

© 2016 by Marina Romani
All rights reserved

Published by
Park Place Publications
Pacific Grove, California
www.parkplacepublications.com

ISBN: 978-1-943887-30-9

Printed in U.S.A
2016

*In memory of Tatiana and Boris Romani, my parents,
who managed to give me a bright and secure childhood
in the midst of extraordinary challenges*

*For Elena, Alex, Shannon, Steve, Vita, Francesca,
Elijah, Madalena, and those who follow*

With deepest gratitude to
- *Lisa Meckel, Alice Tao, Joan Hendrickson,
Christine Pearson Casanave, and the late Anita Alan*
  — *friends, fellow writers, caring readers*

Illia Thompson
  —*friend, fellow writer, first springboard*

Patrice Vecchione
  —*friend, writer extraordinaire, mentor*

With lasting memories of Shurik
  —*my partner in childhood*

Дети — это мира нежные загадки,
И в самих загадках кроется ответ!

Марина Цветаева, «Мирок»

Children are the gentle riddles of our lives,
Concealed within these riddles are the keys!

Marina Tsvetaeva, "Wee World"

Contents

OVERVIEW 1

   A World that Was 1
   Assembling the Memories 2

1. CIRCLING INWARD 5

   ~Shadows –*childhood moments, pre-dream images* . . . 5
   From Tatiana Romani's Diary, June 20, 1939 . . . 5
   Interwoven 6

2. ENTWINING 7

   ~Shadows –*first remembered moments* 7
   Wild Child 7
   Baba Yaga 8
   My Babbi and Me 8
   Feeling Small 9
   ~Shadows–*in the shared house* 11
   Bombs and Pomegranates 12
   Flights with Papa 13
   Rhymes for Papa 14
   ~Shadows –*pictures in the cathedral* 15
   Christmas Venus 16
   Color Burst 17
   America Comes to Shanghai— SPAM, KLIM,
   and Other New Experiences 19
   Lessons 23
   ~Shadows —*midsummer-night adventures* . . . 24
   On Bubbling Well Road 26
   Living Side by Side 27
   Times with Pals 29
   Cicada Summer 31
   ~ *Interlude:* Afternoon Watch 31
   My Grandmother Vera Kirill'na 32

~*Interlude:* Moon Child Dreaming	34
~*Shadows* —*in the hospital*	35
~*Shadows* —*waiting to be well*	35
Summer Train Ride	36
In the Mountains with Papa	37
Tomboy In Silk	39
Boy-Girl, a Dream	40
Stalin and Other Stories in the Roof	41
On My Godfather's Lap	42
The Sacred Heart	44
Arithmetic Class	46
New Girl in Class	47
Herman	48
In Papa's Workshop	49
~ *Interlude:* She Goes with Me	50

3. SPIRALING OUT ... 53

Bezhats—A Talk with Mama	53
~ *Interlude:* A World in Scatters	54
The Doll Barrel	55
From *From Me to You*, by Tatiana Romani, 1996	57
On the S.S. Hwa Lien/Arrival on the Island	58
Tubabao— Snapshots of Memory	59
From *From Me to You*, by Tatiana Romani, 1996	62

4. REVIEWING THE WEAVE ... 65

To My Mother	65
To My Father	65
Always with the Sea	66
Looking Back	67

AFTERWORD — The Next Sixty-Five Years ... 69

OVERVIEW

A World That Was

Shanghai of the 1940s, where I spent the first part of my childhood, was a lively city of many nationalities, where crowded alleyways bustling with vending carts opened up onto western-style avenues upon which bicycles and man-pulled rikshas merged with chauffeur-driven cars, where a large and varied Chinese population intermingled with well-to-do Europeans, Americans, Russian émigrés known as White Russians, and Jewish refugees from Hitler's Germany. That was the scene until 1943, when the Europeans and Americans vanished—most fled leaving all they owned behind; the rest were interned by Japanese occupiers. From that year, all Jewish refugees were confined to a district that became known as the Shanghai Ghetto. —In the early 1940s, Shanghai was a city caught in the middle of a world war, existing under the severe conditions of a foreign occupation. The Japanese were in control. The Europeans and the Americans were gone. The Chinese, the stateless Russians, and the Jewish refugees remained—in various degrees of discomfort.

 I was born in Shanghai in 1939, the only child of Russian parents who, having escaped Communist rule earlier in the century, were part of the large émigré community that, since the 1920s, had established itself within the Chinese international metropolis. My early memories include the years of World War II, air raids, the Japanese occupation, and the city's short post-war period in the midst of China's resurgent Civil War. Then, in 1949, after the Communist takeover of China, we were among several thousand White Russians who, having resisted the Stalinist repatriation drive of the mid-1940s, were evacuated with United Nations help to Tubabao, a remote island in the Philippines, a country then in a close post-war relationship with the United States. There, in dense jungle, the Russian refugees made-do in a makeshift tent city constructed from U.S. Army surplus supplies. After almost a year on Tubabao, my family—my mother, father, grandmother, and I—received immigration papers enabling us to leave for our next home, Sydney, Australia. I was ten. I would turn eleven before we moved on again, to our final destination—the United States—and our family's nomadic period would be over.

Memories of that first decade of my life engendered the poems and prose passages in this collection. They live in a tapestry woven of Russian fairy-tale figures, statues of Confucius, bright prancing dragons, round cathedral domes, intricate pagodas, Western-style department stores, street markets, crowded alleys, and spacious parks dotted with lily ponds. Images of blackouts, air raids, schoolrooms, and games roll out for me to the accompaniment of Chinese English French and Russian speech, alarm sirens, car horns, venders' street calls, and children's chants. The tapestry unrolls to end-of-war celebrations, American soldiers and sailors, riverside ports and ships, high waves and ocean views, green tents and palm trees. I was the child woven into and out of that tapestry, and these writings are my remembrance of a small life within a wider world that has long ago ceased to exist.

Assembling the Memories

My early experiences, as innocent as childhood itself, were inevitably affected by the world in which they took place. It was a world caught in a swirl of dramatic and violent international events, and my reminiscences have their full meaning only against the background of that place and time. Because some of that background may not be generally known, I've woven into my recollections (arranged in loose chronological order) a series of short contextual links— italicized "story captions" that provide information, both autobiographical and historical,[1] that I was mostly unaware of as a child. As well, three short pieces of my mother's writing— an excerpt from her diary and two from her memoir—serve to pinpoint key moments.[2]

A paradox presents itself here: the poems and prose passages that tell the experiences and feelings of a young girl were written down in various moods over a period of several years by me, a woman of advanced age. While the pure voice of the girl that I was rings clearly and always within me, it is inextricably part of the woman that I am today. The result is that, while the child's voice dominates much of the writing, it is often joined by that of the adult she has become. The interweaving thus exists not only on the level of cultural mixes but also in the ebb and flow of time. As my moods shift from memory to memory, corresponding variations occur in my points of view and, especially, in my uses of tense. A conversation of sorts is taking place here, between time past and time present, between child and woman. I have to trust that whoever chooses to ramble with me through my, perhaps eccentric, story-telling ways will accept these mingled voices for what they are—a reflection of the way most of us exist simultaneously in all of our lived selves.

In the end I return with gratitude to members of my larger family. Their voices may not be evident here, but their echoes persist. They come from all those who managed to survive and thrive, in one generation, through two revolutions and two world wars. They could do so, I feel, because of the bonds that held between and among them and because of their will to endure whatever hardships came their way. My parents embodied these qualities for me. This collection intends both to honor them and to keep alive, at least for a little while, our unusual moment within the constantly unpredictable and often frustrating flow of human events. Perhaps it will encourage some to consider what it all meant. And for my family members, perhaps it will also bring on a few smiles of recognition.

---

[1] I have made every effort to verify my statements with research, mostly of Internet sources. But because this collection is built primarily from my early memories and family stories, inaccuracies may have entered; I take full responsibility for those. Chinese place names and personal names appear in the version I remember them, or from my parents' accounts.

[2] My mother's diaries and the memoir she wrote for the family in the last years of her life are in Russian; the excerpts I include here are my translations. As well, most of the conversation fragments that appear in my poems are my renderings, as I remember them, from Russian into English. Any other translations from Russian that appear here, including the epigraph excerpt from a poem by Marina Tsevataeva, are mine.

1. Circling Inward

Shadows — *Childhood moments return like shadows dancing together, as one fades another appears, they mingle, flowing like water, like fog passing through clouds.*

Black, grey on white, coil, fold, expand, contract to slivers, smooth grainy, grainy smooth, slivers coil fold, contract expand in darkness, sleep flows in, soft, till it folds me in.

These pre-dream images persisted throughout my childhood years. Were they birth memories? When did they cease? They've been gone a long time. I'm now old and my mother has died. Two days after she died, I dared to open her diary. As I turned a page, I felt my breath catch—I saw my mother's hand shaping a date two days after she had given birth to me. I read:

From Tatiana Romani's Diary, June 20, 1939

June 20, 1939 — the hospital.

Day before yesterday, I gave birth to a girl, and I'm only now beginning to get used to the thought that I have a daughter, my daughter. It's so strange, incredible, even funny. My soul fills with inexpressible bliss at the thought that this girl is the fruit of the love between me and my own dear Boris, my Bob, my Bus'ka.

Now I love Bob even more, if loving more is possible. I only hope that he'll be able to get truly attached to this little girl and come to love her as much as I do already. I pray to God that this child will bring peace and joy to our home and become the key to a new mutual understanding between me and my beloved Bus'ka.

Sixty-five years after she made that entry, my mother suffered a stroke that would eventually take her life. But first it took away her power of speech. It was then that I lost her.

Interwoven

She has woven herself through my fabric.
She tingles in my toes, throbs in my gut
winds through my veins, tangles in my skull.

I began as a knot in her belly
and she took possession —
as I spread out within, then beyond her
she threaded herself through me
one day at a time, year after year
till at last I seemed on my own.

Now I yearn for the voice on the phone
for the mother who listens
without hearing perhaps, but listens
with pride to this other woman
who bears the mark of her weave.

I am interwoven, in spite of myself.

2. ENTWINING

Our family—my parents, my grandmother Babbi, and I— lived in a large apartment complex in the International Settlement section of Shanghai. When I was one, my mother took me on a vacation to a seaside resort called Tsingtao. By the age of two or three, I had a playmate, but my toddler life was mostly filled with grown-ups, including friends called aunts and uncles.

Shadows — *first remembered moments, Shanghai/Tsingtao*

Mama holds my hand. We walk up to a house. A stranger house. Up steps, through a door. Strangers. Mama lets go of my hand. I don't see her. I open my mouth wide. Cry. Very loud. Drop hot tears.

Soft grass. Shurik is small like me. He's my friend. We hold hands, walk together. Bounce, bounce, up, down, on soft grass. We'll get married when we grow up. Our Mamas laugh when we say that.

I go to Babbi's room. Sit on her lap. Babbi takes me walking.

In earliest childhood, I responded to the adult world with a sense of wonder tinged with fear.

Wild Child

I look out from behind my eyes.
I try to figure things out. They smile at me
tickle my cheek, say silly things,
then they laugh in that special way.
They're all of them bigger than me.
I don't laugh. I'm trying to figure things out.

I have two Uncle Georges.
They call one of them George the Lover
because he acts with Mama in plays.
They call the second one George.
Uncle George, the second one, says

he eats little girls with big bows in their hair.
I have a big bow in my hair.

Every time Uncle George comes over
I climb behind the sofa. He can't get me there.
They laugh. Mama and Papa tell other people
how I hide from Uncle George. They laugh.
I look out from behind my eyes.
Something is happening. I don't understand it.

I want to know why things are.
Mama, why do they laugh when I'm scared?
Mama laughs a little.
You're my little philosopher is all she says.
I'm getting used to being called that.
I'm trying to figure out what that is.

Baba Yaga

She comes out of the stories
stooped Baba Yaga with a sack on her back
filled with the children she'll eat in her shack.
Her bony old fingers reach into my bed,
scraggly nails claw my blanket
raspy voice scratches my air and she croons
— *sweet little one, oh, my maliutka,* she sighs.
I cry out to my grown-ups
they come and turn on the lights
shake out my blanket, point to corners
—*see? all empty!* they say.
They don't see, they don't know,
but *I* know, she is there, in the night.

My Babbi and Me

I like to go to Babbi's room and sit in her lap.
She has a soft fold in the middle of her breast.
I like to stick my finger down there.
It's soft and warm inside.

Babbi makes a stern look, pulls out my finger.
Later I'll try it again. I'm not afraid of her.

One day she puts milk in her coffee and stirs it.
Oh, it's curdled, she says.
Then she looks at me. *Well, we'll just uncurdle it.*
She smiles and stirs the other way.
Now I know how to uncurdle milk.

Sometimes Babbi and I go walking.
We go to the old cemetery
and we look at the stone angels.
My favorite one has big wide wings,
and it smiles over a little girl.
Her face is in a picture on her grave.
I pretend I'm that girl, and the angel
will always watch over me.

Then we walk by a long stone wall
with statues inside its nooks. We count them.
I'm pretty good until twenty-nine.
Then I say, *twenty-ten,* and Babbi frowns.
Twenty-eleven, twenty twelve, I go.

Babbi makes her stern look.
I'm supposed to know
what comes after twenty-nine,
but I like to tease Babbi.
I'm not afraid of her.

Feeling Small

My arms stretched up
my hands high above my head
Mama holds one, Papa holds the other one.
We're walking in the park
their faces smile far, far away.

At school we're called Minims.
The teacher nuns put us into pairs
then hand-in-hand we walk

down long and winding stairs.
The big girls point and giggle as we go.
Oh look, they say, *so cute, those Minims!*
That makes me want to hide.
I'm really big and serious inside.

I look in the mirror and I see a boring face.
All the other girls have something
that makes me notice them,
a turned-up nose or curly lip
or naughty eyes, but I have just a face.
I go to Mama, *Is my face pretty?*
It's a face like a face, she says
—a boring face, she means.
I study the mirror, curl my lip, twist my eyes.
It's no use. I'm stuck with just a face.

I have a hat to match my white and furry coat.
The coat's ok. I hate the hat. It has two peaks.
It makes me look cute, like a bunny.
I never want to wear it, but Mama makes me.
I pound on the bunny peaks to make it round,
more grown-up. I don't like *cute*.

But today is Easter. Mama undoes my pigtails
brushes my hair—it stays curly but hangs loose.
I have a new dress—it's soft and green with white dots.
We go outside. A little wind brushes my face, my hair.
My dress swings against my legs, my legs are bare.
I feel loose, like my dress and my hair. I feel pretty.

In wartime Shanghai, where I spent my early childhood years, Japanese soldiers walked in the streets and American bombs fell from the sky. In this Chinese city, it was the Europeans who had held the power and the money, until the Japanese took over: French and British citizens who didn't manage to get out of the city in time ended up in internment camps. At the same time we, Russian émigrés, were allowed to live more or less as before. As officially "stateless," we were not deemed a threat to the occupiers. It was a time of hardship nevertheless. With the British gone, my father no longer had his job with the British company he had worked for, and Mama and Papa had to improvise ways for us to survive—for a while, Papa delivered coal on his bike; Mama churned soy milk, which Papa also delivered. At one point, Papa and his friends pooled what money they could come up with to buy a car and try to operate a taxi business. None of their entrepreneurial efforts met with much success, but we managed not to go hungry. In the last year of the war, for reasons that were not made clear to me, we moved out of our centrally-located apartment and shared a house with two other Russian families. This place was in the city's outskirts.

Shadows — *in the shared house*

On the garden path, three girls stand beneath a shady tree. We've never seen each other before. I'm the little one. I'm four. Ksana's eight and Lena's ten. We're all going to live in the same house, our family and their two families. Japanese people live in a house nearby. Sometimes I hear them speak. Japanese sounds different from Chinese and Russian. Ksana and Lena know a lot. They show me a broken pomegranate and shiny red beads are inside. Sometimes they tell me stories and riddles, funny ones, different from Mama's. The garden where we play is big, and the grass is so tall it reaches above my tummy. On a hot summer day, the grown-ups burn the grass. It gets short, but it turns black and smells funny. Mama Papa and I live downstairs, but Babbi's not here. I'm standing on the garden path and Mama tells me Babbi has died. I won't see her again. I don't say anything. I won't see Babbi again. I don't know what to do. Long vines grow up the garden wall, in the back corner. We have trees. The one by the veranda has big white flowers. Another one has silk worms, soft white ones, and after a while they curl up into cocoons. I'm not supposed to touch them, but sometimes I do. That's what it's like where we live, on Wuding Road. And there's a war.

Bombs and Pomegranates

I hide inside tall grass near creeping yellow vines
inside the green, below cloud-speckled blue
beneath white magnolia blossoms hanging down
like giant butterflies shivering wings in light wind.

In this big garden we play our games, and here I am
in the grass, where the big girls always find me, laughing.
Later, we sit in the shade of the leafy tree
watch it drop round pomegranate bulbs
—they crack and spill red beads, so fun to touch and taste.

Bedtime is too soon, but Mama's bunny story makes it cozy.
It's a different story every night, but it always ends the same
—*Fluffy tucks Muffy and Puffy into their pink and blue cots
and kisses them good night.* Mama and I kneel. We say,
kind God, please keep us safe and make the war stop.
Mama gives me a kiss and tiptoes out.

I curl up under cool soft covers and close my eyes.
I think about war, a scary thing, a jumble of ugly colors
—grey and brown and black, like air raids and blackouts.
When sirens sound, we turn down lights, pull drapes tight.
Airplanes fly above. They drop bombs, sometimes nearby.

When Papa bikes me to kindergarten we go in the street
and ugly colors—people, bikes, rikshas, grey, black, brown,
all move, roll forward like the river. Then a siren screams
and it's all splashes, people running—up, down, around.
Papa lifts me off his bike and we stand in a doorway.
I want to go, but he makes me stay there till the *all-clear*.

Some days Mama takes me to the market. It's a noisy soup.
Wet smells of cabbage-apple-chicken-straw
soggy mishmash of green-red-yellow all stirred up
in talking-shouting-squawking. I carry my small basket
just like Mama's, and the fruit man smiles, puts in an apple.
Walking home, Mama holds my hand, keeps us moving.
But I see it on the sidewalk. The swaddled baby.
It lies alone. Its grey still face. Black flies, crawling.

Despite the difficult circumstances in which we lived, my parents, each in their own way, managed to give me a sweet and secure childhood. My father expressed his affection indirectly, through story-telling and fun. He was a kind, patient man, and I remember only one instance in which he lost his temper with me.

Flights with Papa

He can stand on his head
he walk on his hands
he can make me fly.
He holds my right hand and my right leg
twirls me around and around.
That's what flying is. Really.
As soon as he walks in the door
I want him to stand on his head,
walk on his hands, make me fly.
Mama laughs, *Papa's been working all day
he's too tired to play.* But he does.
He does it and smiles.

Sometimes he tells me stories at bedtime.
The best ones are about when he was a boy.
I've heard some of them again and again.
When he reads to me, he picks adventure books.
Some are about brave girls. I like those best.

He never yells. He never gets mad. Except once he did.

I didn't want to eat the borscht. First it was too hot.
Then it wasn't, but a fat white film spread on top.
My spoon got coated with the ickky white film.
They said I couldn't get up till I finished the borscht.
I sat and I sat. I didn't want to eat the borscht.
I picked up my spoon, I put it down. I was bored.

I wiggled. I turned my head to the back of my chair.
The chair back has little wooden pictures
—an eagle with two heads and one crown on top,
a knight on a horse poking a spear into a dragon,
some funny curvy shapes. The pictures are fun.

I started making up a story about the knight.
I forgot about the borscht.

Voices of grown-ups floated up, got fuzzy.
My special little fork was still next to my plate
from when I ate the cutlet, before the borscht came.
I picked it up and turned myself all the way around.
I stuck the fork tip into the wood. It was soft.
I started tracing a funny shape. So much to do.

Ooof! I felt my Papa's foot hit my bottom.
I flew out of my chair, all the way to the living room.
No more sitting. No more carving. No more borscht.

That's how mad my Papa got once.

My father enjoyed writing verse, and sometimes he wrote poems especially for me—these were rhymed narratives, either about episodes in his own childhood or in mine. The poems, in their original Russian, survive among my memorabilia. The following tribute to him is my belated thank you note.

Rhymes for Papa

When I was small you took the time
to write story-poems for me in rhyme.
So just for you, and just this time,
I'll rhyme for you, I'll be sublime.

•

All snuggled in bed I'd wait to hear
your memory sing, make pictures appear.
Visions of Russia long ago —
three white horses race through snow.

The family sits bundled up in the sleigh,
they're out for a ride on this dazzling day.
Your dashing Papa, reins firmly in hand,
runs his troika on whitened land.

But, oops! By speed he's been carried away,
and down on its side goes the family sleigh.

Brother sister Mama roll and spill out.
Nanny's stuck —in the snowdrift! comes a shout.

Scuffles, laughter, snow brushed away,
Nanny's rescued. *Let's be on our way!*
Not so fast, grumbles she, preparing to scold,
Y'almost killed me, you fool! I'm near' hundred years old!

•

Stories in verse and stories in prose,
too many to tell at one time, I suppose.
Stories of school days, of pals, and of pranks,
and visits with friends on a river's banks.

Those memory songs told what was before
Russia was torn by revolt and by war,
before bloodshed and famine and civil strife
ended forever your childhood life.

You fled your country, left all behind,
a home and a life in a new world to find.
But your humor and decency no ordeal could destroy,
and times spent with you came with laughter and joy.

My father. My Papa. In your own gentle way
you set the standard I'll never betray.
Mama worked hard to make a good me,
yet by watching you I knew how to be.

My mother was the moralist—kind or stern depending on the situation. Russian Orthodoxy was at the foundation of her beliefs, and it guided her both in the conduct of her life and in the way she tried to raise me.

Shadows — *pictures in the cathedral*

The cathedral is a big big place. I stand next to Mama, and people are standing all around—beside us, in front of us, behind us. They're all looking at the altar. That's where the bishop is. I hear the choir singing above, somewhere I can't see. I can't see the altar either because I'm short and the other people are tall. I look at the backs of their coats and the backs of their knees. The coats are a little bit wet from the rain so they have that funny wet-dog smell. In between some coats and knees, I spot a girl my size, maybe a little bit bigger. I can see *her* face because she's turned around, away from the altar. She's very serious, I wonder what she's looking at. I study her, I try to figure her out. She notices me and screws up her face, quickly looks down at her dress—*what's wrong with it?* she seems to ask, to let me know, I guess, that I'm not supposed to stare. I turn away as fast as I can.

Better to look up, into the big dome. I drop my head back and, all the way up there, I see God. He's huge, he wears something loose and blue, he has long white hair and a big white beard. His arms are spread out, like he wants to hold all of us safe. Angels are all around him—the singing, maybe it's not the choir. Maybe it's coming from the angels' mouths up there, in that beautiful dome. So I keep looking up. And it's all right.

Christmas Venus

reflections on a late-December evening
sometime in the 21st century, in Monterey, California

Pine silhouettes pierce a canvas of silver
a sky lit by the fullest of moons
while Venus ripples in sonorous silence.
Houses twinkle with red green and blue
lights of Christmas, yet it's Venus aglow
that beckons me back to the magic created
by Mama long long ago, light years away.

On Christmas Eve morning we started a fast
and waited all day for the first star to appear.
Its light marked the renewal of a mystery —
the birth of a promise made two millennia ago.
While stars marked the night sky, we stood at vespers
in darkness touched only by flickering candles
and incense flowing through chanting and song.

Then home to a holiday dinner with a dessert
made of wheat berries, honey, and nuts —
in memory of ancients who prayed through the night
then broke fast with this simplest of meals.
And at last, I curled up with my dreams
of tomorrow, Saint Nick, and the doll he might bring.

Tomorrow happened as promised: bright gifts
were piled up beneath a candle-lit fir, and, yes,
the white-whiskered Saint Nick, who drove up
in a jingling sleigh —or, a sled pulled by Papa?
A show staged with care for me and my friends
by parents contending with wartime and shortage
in an occupied city, long long ago, light years away.

And tonight, watching Venus sing silent
in silver pierced by long shadows of pines
I stand in the light of a night of my childhood
when mystery met magic and my small soul came aglow.

One day the war was over. The Japanese left quickly, and our life changed overnight. We returned to our apartment in the International Settlement —on Bubbling Well Road, in a complex called Garden Apartments. My memories of the early post-war days are marked by excitement, color, and light.

Color Burst

Standing with my finger in my mouth in the middle of the dining room on an ordinary day, I was pondering what to do with myself, when Mama walked into the room smiling. She told me our prayers had been answered: the war was over. Everything around me felt the same, yet I sensed something important had happened, that I needed to produce a reaction. I smiled as brightly as I could and made a happy little skip. It was the best I could do at that moment. Then the changes came. Visibly, rapidly.

Before I knew it, we were back in our apartment. Shanghai was jubilant—the city burst into color overnight, and end-of-war celebrations were everywhere. My pals—Shurik, Irina, Ronnie — were there, in Garden Apartments, too. As young as we all were, we felt the excitement, were enchanted by it. We were by now allowed to run around the complex without supervision, and we gathered every day at the complex's main gate, where a ledge at the top accommodated the four of us. We'd clamber up and huddle together, looking out over the wide sweep of Bubbling Well Road where, at a broad intersection, stood a massive victory arch. It rose as high as the buildings around it, packed with bright paper flowers in and around intricate ornaments and scrolls, all of it and pulsing with color—green, orange, red, white, black, bright yellow. At the center of this construction, enormous portraits of Chiang Kai-shek and Dr. Sun Yat-sen looked out at the city in grim triumph. We didn't for a moment doubt that *they*, these heroes of the world we lived in, had won the war single-handedly.

Curled up on our ledge, our vantage point, we'd gaze at this display for a while and then we'd run off to play. When the dragon dancers came, we ran back. Day after day they came. We always heard them coming—the drums, the many-toned clang of cymbals, the dragons prancing. Thumping, thrumming, clanging, sweeping red and orange, swishing yellow white and blue, and the giant-headed, many-footed dragons bounding, playing, dancing, leaping joy. And always the crowds gathered round.

The dragon was wide awake, and Chinese movie-making was waking up with it. Along the big streets, movie billboards sprang up—gigantic tableaus of men and women embracing, men wielding knives, faces grimacing in horror, blood flowing. These scenes held little meaning for me, and I sensed I wouldn't be seeing those movies. But the colorful pictures in the sky looked out at me out of the blackness I had associated with the city during all the years of my life up to that point. They captivated me as I sat with Mama in a pedicab, and one evening after nightfall, I saw neon for the first time ever. There, high above us, mounted on a tall dark building, was an oblong sign all lit up with green Chinese characters running down the middle, and tiny red stars were flickering around its border, racing, skipping over each other, around and around, leaving me spellbound.

Before long, neon lights of every color would flood the city and I'd stop being surprised by them. But those first skippy stars still live in me as harbingers of something completely new and magical.

Once the Japanese had left, the Americans started arriving. We watched the giant ships move along the Huangpu River, and the sailors and soldiers crowded on deck looking out at our city, watching us watching them. Then, almost overnight, America seemed everywhere around us.

America Comes to Shanghai — SPAM, KLIM, and Other New Experiences

1.
Sailors and soldiers walk around the streets.
The sailors' wear uniforms with big collars,
blue with white. The soldiers wear ugly green.
They're called GI's. They act loud
especially when they call out to girls —
the big girls, almost grown up, like ladies.
Some of them are Chinese, some Russian,
they wear bright make-up, fancy clothes.
Their families are often angry at them
because they go with soldiers, act in new ways,
but their families can't stop them.

At home we have different food now.
A lot of it comes from the black market
in cans the same ugly green as GI uniforms.
There's meat called SPAM, and yummy grape juice.
Also powdered milk. It's in yellow cans
with the letters KLIM on them.
I've figured out that's *milk* spelled backwards.
I don't like klim much, but I have to drink it.
 —we couldn't get milk during the war,

so my teeth have cavities.
Now I have to drink klim for my teeth.

We have bubble gum too—it's pink!
Mama had to teach me how it works
— you chew it until it gets soft
then you stretch your tongue into it
and blow until you get a bubble.
Once it's soft, you can also pull it out
into a pink string and make shapes.
It's fun, especially outside with my friends
—we see who can make the biggest bubble
or pull out the longest gum string.

But comic books are the most fun.
My pals and I like the ones about
Captain Marvel and Mary Marvel
and Captain Marvel Junior
—they start out as regular people
but become magic when they say *Shazam!*
Then they get super strong and fly around
and beat up bad people and save the world.
We read our comic books all the time,
then we make up games where we pretend
to be the Marvels. We spread our arms
and run fast, so it looks like we're flying.
We fight evil everywhere, just like they do.

2.
One day, we visited American friends in a camp.
It's called an internment camp.
It has a high fence around it. The Japanese
made them live there while the war was on.
They don't have to stay there anymore.
The gates are open, but people are still there.
Maybe they're waiting to go home to America.
In the camp, I saw a man with black skin.
I've never seen anyone like that before.
He was playing baseball. I've never seen baseball
before either. It looks kind of like cricket

but the bat is round and thick, and people run
around bases instead of running back and forth.
I saw the black man hit the ball with the round bat.
People were cheering, so I think he was good at it.
The other thing I saw at the camp was a big hole
in the ground. People said it's where a bomb fell.
I remembered the air raids and the blackouts.
The hole was deep. I just stood there looking.

3.
Ships called tankers are on the Huangpu.
They carry oil to a terminal on Pudong,
a big place on the other side of the river.
American companies own the oil.
One of them is called Socony.
Their emblem is on a lot of billboards
— a red horse with wings.
Papa works at a different one, Caltex.
I like their emblem better. I can draw it
—a red star with CALTEX across it.
I do it over and over in my sketch book.

When Papa is working at the terminal
I get to visit sometimes. The oil is inside
huge round storage tanks as tall as houses.
They have skinny ladders running up the side,
so you can climb all the way to the top.
I'm afraid, a little, but I hold my breath and go.
I get to the top, look down: the grass is far below
it feels like something is pulling me to jump off.
I start to get dizzy. I turn away quickly.

Other times, Papa works on a tanker on the river.
Then we don't see him for a few days
because he sleeps on the ship. He writes poems there.
Every time he comes home, he brings me a new one.
Some of the poems are about him and Aunt Vera
when they were children. Some are about me.
Some are stories he makes up, but I'm still in them.

They're usually funny, but some are supposed to
teach me things —about good manners, or patience.
I don't like those so much.

4.
Because there isn't any more war,
we can go to places outside the city.

Once we went to the harbor
where the Americans keep their ships.
They have a machine called an LST.
It's a car and a boat at the same time.
We got a ride on one. It was OK while it felt
like a car, sort of crawling, but it kept going
toward the water's edge and it crawled right in
into deep water, and I was sure we'd drown.
My heart went all the way down to my feet.
I've never been so scared. I tried not to show it.

Another time we went to the sea—it's far!
We rode in a car with our friends
and I thought we'd never get there.
At last, I saw sand and lots of water.
It was yellow, just like the Huangpu.
In pictures the sea is always blue
so I thought this was still the river
but the grown-ups said it was the sea.
We put on swimsuits in a little house
and went down to the beach.
I started running fast — I wanted to jump
right into the water, but it was too low!
We had to walk and walk and walk.
The sand under my feet felt ripply and hard
and the water never got higher than my belly.
Then Mama taught me to bounce on the waves
and it didn't matter any more about the water,
that it was shallow and yellow.
I wanted to stay in it forever.

From the time I was six years old, I went to a Catholic English-speaking girls' school, the Convent of the Sacred Heart. At first, my classmates were mostly children of "Europeans," Russian émigrés included —i.e., Caucasians—and a sprinkling of wealthy Chinese girls. American girls would start to appear a bit later, after American families started arriving in the city. The nuns operated a separate Chinese-speaking school in a building nearby, where their teaching apparently followed the traditional Chinese approach—rote learning; we could hear the children chanting their lessons on the other side of our schoolyard.

When I started going to this school, I knew no English because my early education, started at home by my mother, included some false starts.

Lessons

Lines, lines on paper. Pencil tight
in my hand, I make strokes and circles —
stroke, stroke, stroke, stroke, start a new line
circle, circle, circle, circle, start a new line
—the page fills up slowly, so slowly.
Russian kindergarten. Long tables. Girls.
Purple uniforms. Milochka's the teacher.
At recess we play catch, tease each other
then start ugly words about the teacher.
I get brave, say out loud, *Milochka is,*
take a breath—*garbage!* My friend who's mean
stares, makes a scary look. *I'll tell! I'll tell!*
I beg and cry, *Please please don't tell! Please please!*
Then she forgets, I guess. We go back inside,
back to lines of strokes, lines of circles.
Stroke, stroke, stroke, circle, circle, circle.

Mama says she will teach me herself.
I think she doesn't like my kindergarten.

Her head is bent low over me, I read slowly,
Sasha eats kasha, Masha eats kasha, Pasha eats kasha.
Then I write the words. Mama's stays close.
All I see is her eyebrow, her cheek, a bit of hair.
She watches my hand make the letters.
I can't wait to get out, play outside.

Now I can read and I can write
and Mama says it's time for French.
Uncle Zhenia comes to teach me French.
I count: *un – deux –trois – quatre.*
I sing: *trois poules vont* to the park,
frère Jacques, bells ring *din din don.*

The letters are different from Russian.
I learn them. I'll go to French school soon.

•

Well, I'm six and I won't go to French school
after all. I'm too old for their first grade.
Sacred Heart will let me into first grade
so that's where I'll go. Mama tells me about it
—the teachers are nuns, they speak English.
The tailor makes me the school uniform
—blue skirt, white blouse, blue necktie.
Papa teaches me to make the knot.
I get good at it, like a boy. I'm proud of that.
I'll learn English letters next.

My new teacher's name is Mother Robaire.
She wears black all over, even on her head,
except she has white ruffles round her face.
I like her face. She takes me to my place.
I have my own desk, like all the other girls.
They sit on both sides of me, in front of me,
behind me. Mother Robaire walks to the front,
her loose black dress swings with her steps.
On a big black board, she makes bright white
letters: C A T . I know those letters! — CAT!
CAT. CAT. I can read that! English will be easy!

Shadows —*midsummer-night adventures*

It's steamy hot, it's not even dark yet, but it's bedtime, they say.
Mama's just finished telling me tonight's bunny family story.
It's fun and it's nice, but I like it better when Papa tells a
bedtime story. He has lots of true ones about when he was in
military boarding school, mostly about how he got himself into

trouble. He was a mischievous boy, he tells me, and I listen admiringly. Not that I could ever get away with crowing like a rooster in the school hallway, or putting lizards under the teacher's desk. I'd be too scared of Mama. Anyway, story-time is over. We've prayed, and I got my good-night kiss. Now I'm supposed to fall asleep. Easy for them to say.

I lie here. Somewhere above, a mosquito's whistling — in a high whiney way. I know he's circling, ready to drop and sting me! I'll try to slap him, but he might get me first. It's hot. I'm sticky. My little white nightshirt is damp. I put my bare feet up on the smooth cool wall, pretend to walk up. I study my scabby brown knees. The windows are open. Sticky warm air drifts in. A baby's crying somewhere. Alley cats are screaming at each other, up on the big wall probably. They do that every night. Sometimes I can't tell if they're cats or babies. Grown-up voices call out something I don't get. I listen. I lie here. I count to twenty. Should I go for a hundred? I get to twenty-eight, twenty-nine. This is boring.

I close my eyes. It's all just grey inside my eyelids. But if I press a little, I can get red, blue, purple, and — oh, look! — now the colors are swirling into pools and circles. I can let go now because green and yellow sparkles are dancing on their own. If I can just keep my eyes closed, and stay awake, I'll have a whole kaleidoscope inside my eyes! I need to stay awake! Green blue yellow sparkles flit in swirly circles, spirals spinning into gold and silver stars. I'm flying inside them, above the mosquitoes, above the hot mists and the night sounds, floating on cool white clouds, swooping in the shiny black sky, dropping into swirling purple pools, swimming silver seas, falling, drowning in a dark and golden deep.

Inside the deep deep deep, I hear *Marii-nik. Marii-nik*—Mama's voice, calling in that singing, morning way of hers. My room is full of light, the sun is shining.

As I was assembling my memories, I began to wonder why the urban street we lived on had its name—no bubbling well there that I knew of. Thanks to the Internet, and help from my friend Alice Tao, I was able to piece together some of its story.

On Bubbling Well Road

1.

Long ago
a spring bubbled from the earth where a temple stood.
The temple by the spring was a serene place
and the people called it Jing An Si
which expressed the peaceful feeling.

For centuries
the spring bubbled and the temple stood
and the Shanghai people cared for the temple.
Then na'kuni traders came in ships with cannons.
They went deep into the land
and they built roads, bridges, and buildings.

Before long
a smooth wide road led to the temple
and Jing An Si was not as peaceful as it once was
but it still stood by the bubbling spring
and the Shanghai people called the new road
Jing An Si Lu, after the temple.
But the na'kuni called the new road
Bubbling Well Road, after the spring.

Soon
the na'kuni filled up the spring
and put buildings where water once bubbled
and after a while the Shanghai people forgot about the spring.
Still they called the road Jing An Si Lu,
and still the na'kuni called it Bubbling Well Road.

2.

My pals and I pass summer days on an island of grass
and tall trees between stone-columned buildings
on Bubbling Well Road—where all of us live.

In hours of sunlight, this is our green island kingdom.
Here we're spinners of tales—warriors, heroes, makers
of magic — here, whatever we dream up is true.

Across the stone wall sound chants in Chinese
—children singing words we don't understand.
Pi'ling pala'a chi, chant the children.
Can they be playing the same game we play
swinging arms back and forth, calling out
stone, paper, scissors before throwing a sign
—fist closed or palm open or two-finger scissors?

We don't know
what they do, we don't go where they live
but they walk in a group by our island sometimes
gazing and pointing at us, stopping to chant.
Na'kuni, na'kuni, chant the children and point.
We pause in our playing not sure what to do.
The children pass by, we go on with our game.

So we live, so we play, side by side yet apart,
aware of each other, unknowing, unknown.

Of course the life of China, in all its variety, was everywhere around us, as were the difficult realities of the city. Sights of poverty and deprivation were ubiquitous and they, inevitably, became embedded in our young consciousnesses.

Living Side by Side

I know one Chinese family that lives in Garden Apartments. Well, I know one person in that family. Hua-ling is an older girl, almost grown up. She likes me and invites me over sometimes. Her parents just smile when I come in. Hua-ling gives me little treats, and she teaches me to say Chinese words. Their apartment has beautiful things—pictures on the walls I like to look at. But we don't do much together, and I don't stay long.

Mostly, Chinese people live in places we never go, but we see them in the streets. A lot of Chinese children's clothes are stuffed with cotton—it keeps the cold out. Sometimes bits of cotton come out of holes in their jackets. Old women wear the same kind of clothes, and they walk funny on their tiny feet in pointed shoes. They go along with the children, take quick small steps and talk fast, like they're scolding them.

The streets are busy, noisy—everybody's going somewhere, carrying something. People walk, talk, argue. Vendors call out names of things they sell from carts — hot food or sweet food —I always want to try their sticky-looking fried twists, but Mama won't ever buy them. She says they're not clean, bad for me.

And there are beggars, especially in the busiest places. Beggars wear rags, all grey, maybe just old and dirty. Some of them have no legs—only stubs—they roll around on small flat carts, pushing off with their hands if they have them. Some have ugly running sores on their skin, purple or dark red. They beg alone or in groups, maybe families. The boys and girls have the same kind of sores. They beg, too. When they see us, they stretch out their hands. That means they need money. If we're in a riksha or pedicab, we ride by. If we're walking, Mama usually gives them something, but she doesn't look at them. I ask about their sores. Mama says they make them on purpose so we'll give them money. I think that would hurt a lot—and scary to have sores like that, just to get money.

Mama is teaching me not to pay attention. She says Chinese people don't feel pain the same way we do. I try to remember that when I see those boys and girls.

Mama's lessons, I now believe, were meant to shelter me from distress, but it took me half a lifetime and a period of living in another Asian country to unlearn them. During childhood, I more or less absorbed the lessons, just as my playmates apparently did, from their own parents—our games took no account of the lives around us.

Times with Pals

Ma-a-ri-i-i-na-a. Ma-a-ri-i-na-a. The sing-song voice outside the window, the call to come out and play, and before I remember asking Mama for permission, I'm out there, with the boys, running, clambering up our tree to the stone wall, where we sit and fantasize in a world known just to us, a world no grown-up can enter. More often than not, the call comes from Shurik, who lives upstairs in our building. He's my best friend. We've played together from when we were little—our mamas remember how we sat side by side in our strollers when they or our *amahs* took us out for walks. We tell each other stuff no one else knows. When the other boys aren't around, he comes over and plays dolls with me. That's a deep secret of his, and I keep it because I like playing dolls with him.

Outside where we play, we have our small gang of friends. Ronnie, from the next building, is a couple of years younger than us, a redheaded freckled Jewish boy we expect we'll convert to Russian orthodoxy. Cheerfully he goes along with our preaching, and our games. His serious-looking parents don't know about our conversion plans. They and Ronny's baby sister Frida come to our birthday parties, and they invite us to theirs. Kenny comes over from across the wall. His mother is Korean, he tells us, and his father is an American. *Over the wall* is where Chinese people live—we've never been there, we've never seen Kenny's family or his home. Shurik, Marina, Ronnie, Kenny. That's us.

Sometimes Irina shows up, from the building across the roadway. Irina and I don't share girl interests much—we both like the boy games. I especially like being told that I'm almost as good as a boy (at home I do exercises in front of the mirror, secretly, to build up my biceps), but Irina is still stronger and faster than me. Irina and I have something like an enemy-friendship. How did that start? Maybe it was always that way. One time, after we quarreled, she went off and started telling the boys she was going to beat me up. The boys warned me and looked out for me, but she found me when no one else was around. I saw her coming and I was scared. She started shooting angry eyes at me, swinging her arms, punching my face and shoulders. I stood there wincing, waiting for it to be over. Soon she stopped. I think I was a boring victim. We went back to our enemy-friendship, and we never talked about the beating.

Irina's older brother Alik is a fat boy we put up with. When we feel nice we call him Polecat— because that sounds kind of like his last name. Other times we call him Fattycum-Banana. We let him join our games, but sometimes we tease him and chant fat-boy chants at him; that's when he's Fattycum-Banana. Irina and Alik's parents own a fur shop on Bubbling Well Road. They're not friendly with our parents, but I've been to their apartment. On hot days they walk around the rooms and eat dinner in their underwear. When I eat with them I keep my clothes on. Once Irina and I played with her miniature doll babies—they're made of celluloid which has a strange sweet smell. That's a girl thing we did together.

When we're not sitting on the wall, we play in the long garden —it's like an island in the middle of the roadway that runs around our buildings. We play cops and robbers, or war, or just "catch," when the person who is "it" has to catch someone who then becomes "it" and it keeps going that way. On rainy days we meet in the large entry hall of the building where Shurik and I live. There we read and trade comic books, usually about the Marvel family, and when the rain stops we play games outside again, pretending we're Captain Marvel, Mary Marvel, and Captain Marvel Junior—that's Shurik, me, and Ronny. We plan to cut out and send in the coupons that come in the comic books to a place in America called Culver City, so we can become members of the Captain Marvel Fan Club. Then we'll get our member cards and our uniforms (Mary Marvel for me!), but we haven't done it yet.

When our mamas start calling us to come inside, we're never ready. We have to go in, but we'll be back tomorrow.

I was my parents' only child, and even though I had a steadfast group of playmates, I learned early to enjoy my solitary times.

Cicada Summer

I lie on green grass
encircled by concrete
on my island of summer

cicadas sound all around
around me cicadas sing zinging

my arms legs bared to the sun
grass blades tickle my skin
cicada shells crackle beneath

I lie still listening watching
acacia tree leaves flicker
in clearest sky blues brushed
light by cloud wisps wafting

summer stillness summer song
green glints yellow-green blue-green
in white-kissed blues acacia flecks
float weave rings in sun shafts
and the golden cicadas are zinging

When my paternal grandmother, Babbi, died, just before the end of the war, I was not taken to her funeral. Probably I was thought too young, and I didn't grasp the magnitude of my loss until much later. It was after I first saw the funeral of a family friend, some years later, that I began to sense the meaning and impact of death. I then became preoccupied with the possibility of losing my mother

Interlude: Afternoon Watch

The child watches her sleeping—
mother lies on her side, eyes closed
her cheek a soft pink, a slight motion
of skin on her throat assures the child
that she breathes, that she lives.

Uncle's face, she remembers,
was white and still in the coffin.
He's the one who always came in
with a smile but now he was still,
silent, eyes closed, mouth shut tight,
and aunt stood beside him in tears
because his smile was no more
and he never again would sit up
or stand up or tell silly stories
or laugh at things that we said.

The child moves in close, climbs up
on the bed as she studies her mother.
What will she do if she dies, if the eyes
she knows to be blue with warm light
remain closed, the moist rosy mouth
never kiss or say that she loves?

The child does not wish to be seen
watching her mother so close. She climbs
carefully down and picks up her book,
turns bright pages, pretending to read.
She waits patient for mother to wake.

Not long after the end of the war and our family's return to Bubbling Well Road, my mother's mother, who had been in a mental institution for several years, came to live with us.

My Grandmother Vera Kirill'na

She was
    the one we saw now and then in the garden of a tall building
    when she came out dressed all in white, and I was four,
    whom I was told to call Busia, a Russian grandmother name,

    the one we later saw in a big ugly room with lots of beds
    where messy wild-eyed women sat around or walked about
    saying things I didn't understand but knew were strange,
    and Mama said we had to take her home, and I was six,

    the one we made room for,
    who now declared she was too young to be a Busia
    and from then on I was to use her patronymic,
    so she was Vera Kirill'na to me ever after.

She was
    the one who always hummed the same little tune
    and could play five pieces on the piano,
    who they said was a wonderful musician once,
    the one I had to share piano time with,

    the one they said used to be a great beauty
    with a thick braid that reached all the way to her waist,
    who now tied up her bits of hair in funny ribbons
    and wore skirts on top of skirts, untucked shirts hanging out.

She was
    the one who talked about people living in the ceiling
    or above it maybe, and they all had names,
    and Mama said I was not to listen when she talked like that,

    the one who sounded angry sometimes and raised her voice
    then would stop and giggle about some joke that was just hers
    and go back to humming that same little tune.

She was
    the one no one loved except Mama,
    whom Papa called his cross in life,
    who was always around, mostly in her cluttered room,
    but appeared in the dining room at odd times of day or night,
    the other member of our family, who was in it but not of it,

    my mother's mother who outlived my father by twelve years
    and in the end had to live among strange people again
    because Mama couldn't lift her anymore,
    who in the last decade of her life stopped speaking entirely.

She was
    my only living grandmother for more than forty years,
    the one I was afraid of although she never touched me,

the one with whom I never had a real conversation,
the forgotten one, whose pink marble gravestone is inscribed
BLESSED ARE THE MEEK
the words chosen by Mama, the only one who knew her.

Although games with playmates now dominated my days, I continued my solitary dreamings.

Interlude: Moon Child Dreaming

The child often had friends around her.
They were dear to her and she liked
spending time with them—in fact, once
she got started, you couldn't tear her away.

Yet that was a problem somehow. In the midst
of it all she didn't know who she was exactly.
Leaving a party or a game or a pastime was hard,
but once out, she floated and flew, and she knew . . .

she knew how trees grow, what the wind sings,
why Mozart's music sparkles, what love says,
and how light reflects on still water in a pool
so deep and dark it glows—she looked in
and found shimmers of an eye, a smile, a face,
and she knew she was seeing the moon-mother,
the one who holds all mysteries inside herself.

The child knew all this while she was alone,
and she knew her own name,
and why she was named that.

Then she was with her friends again
and she loved them, but what she had known
in her solitude broke up and scattered,
and she could not fit the pieces together.

I was about eight when I heard the adults talking about outbreaks of meningitis in the city. In our little crowd, Shurik was the first to be diagnosed with the disease. I came down shortly afterwards. This was a time when penicillin was just beginning to be used to treat this dangerous illness, and it's likely that we both owed our complete recovery to that fact.

Shadows—*in the hospital*

Black. I'm inside the black. Black all around. I float inside the black. Deep. Dark. Oozy. But there's a little red patch. Shining. It's me. I know it is. I have to go there, get into it. It's hard because it's small, and it glows and floats, and black is all around. Floats away. Red glow floats in black. So hard. I have to find the way in. Into the red shine. Through the black. So hard. I'm trying, struggling to get into the shiny red patch. . . .

In a bed. Not my bed. The hospital. Not allowed to get up. Somebody brings me food, and I have stay in bed while I eat. Different people come in and give me shots. Shots all day long. My bumbum hurts. They keep poking it. Mama comes in. She talks to me or she reads to me. Then she talks to the day nurse. The day nurse is the nice one. She lets Mama stay as long as she wants. The night nurse is very strict. Mama says she's a witch. She makes Mama leave. She's always angry about something. I'm scared of her. I want to go home.

The treatment involved being injected with penicillin every three hours. After my hospital stay, I spent quite a long time—it felt like several weeks—at home in bed. By then, the frequency of injections must have been reduced, but a nurse came in every day.

Shadows—*waiting to be well*

Every time the nurse comes in I know I'm going to be hurt. As soon as I see her I start arguing where the shots will go: *left side, no right side, no left side.* Both my sides hurt a lot, but I argue. Anything to keep her from starting. Finally, I have to pull down my pajamas and roll over. She starts poking. The penicillin goes in first. But it's not the worst one. Now she gets out the big glass tube and her long needle. It's for the liver shot. She and Mama say it will make me strong again. In goes the needle and I feel the thick stuff ooze into me, slow, slow down from the poking place through the inside of my bumbum, inch after inch after inch. I try to be brave, but I make moaning noises. Then I count out loud, I mean I *yell* out loud — ONE, TWO, . . . by the time I get to TEN, I know it's getting close to the end. Still I keep asking *when, when?* At last, it's over, and the nurse goes away. I stay in bed.

The rest of the time I don't mind it so much. I get to eat things I like. Chicken. Mashed potatoes. I play with the mashed potatoes, and Mama doesn't stop me. I think she doesn't look. I work my fork to shape the white mush into hills and fortresses, then I make up stories about battles in the hills and things like that. Mama and Papa read to me more than they usually do. We've almost finished *Little Women*. I like that book a lot. Jo is my favorite character. She's a girl but she can act like a boy, and she writes plays that she and her sisters act out. I started writing a book before I got sick, and I might be a writer when I grow up. I think I'm a lot like Jo.

For the final part of my recovery, the doctor said that I should spend some time away from the city. Fresh air and lots of exercise was what he prescribed. My father then took two weeks off from work, and he and I went by train to Moganshan, a mountain resort about 200 kilometers southwest of Shanghai.

Summer Train Ride

somewhere between Shanghai and Moganshan

fields flow by my window
rice plants water drenched
long blades liquid green
stir in sunlight, bend and glow
we roll through green flow
train wheels click below
click tak tak tak, click tak tak

out there, men, women
here now, there now
feet bare, trousers rolled
bend low, bow to rice blades
a buffalo lolls in river shallows
browns blend in muddy yellows

atop the buffalo a boy dozes
underneath water crawls low
ripples slow along long fields

fields stream on, the train passes
leather seats creak, crick crack
amber tea sways, glows in glasses
tea sways, seats creak, train rolls
click tak tak tak, click tak tak

In the Mountains with Papa

Fog clouds rise through bamboo and pine,
in evening coolness grown-up voices hum
on the hotel veranda, as I sit quiet near Papa
looking at fog mist, thinking of mountains.

I loved mountains before I ever saw a real one
because Nina, my hero in *Princess Dzhavaha*,
was a girl who lived in the high Caucasus.
She cantered her beloved Shahly
through gorges and peaks and had adventures.
Nina, Shahly, and mountains engrossed me.
I'll run to the first mountain I see and I'll hug it,
I said to myself. But that didn't happen.

•

We rode on a train and the land was flat
with rice fields forever, I thought.
Later new shapes, like mounds,
showed up on the horizon line.
Slowly they grew, and then we were there
by the mountains of Moganshan,
and I saw nothing I could ever hug.
It was all too big: land rising to somewhere,
and trees—*pines*, Papa said, and *bamboo*.
It was nothing like my book or my dreams.

Canopied chairs on long poles stood near
the foot of a mountain, waiting for people like us,
and coolies came over, offering to carry us up.

We would sit, Papa in one chair, I in the other,
while the coolies grasping the poles on each end
would carry us to the place we needed to go.
Papa bargained a price, the carriers threw lots
about who would take me because I was light,
and then off we went in a sprinkle of rain,
our chairs draped in oilcloth to protect us
from rain and the chill, swaying gently,
one-two, to the tap of men's feet as they treaded
in rhythm the tiny stone steps that were carved
in the mountain, all the way to the top.

•

Our time there passed quickly.
As we walked on paths along ridges
grown thick with bamboo and pine, I swung
the cane Papa made me and taught me to use.
Tiered airy pagodas and squatty stone shrines
often rose on our way— a part of the forest
they seemed, and pretty surprises for us
as we trekked to a pool surrounded by stone
for afternoon swims in its clear deep coolness.

One day, another surprise—we met
Shurik and his Mama at a nearby hotel.
Now the two of us joyfully played, climbed,
and swam together in the long afternoons.

Evenings—sunsets above the ravine,
sitting quiet with Papa and friends
watching fog drift through the trees,
feeling the cooling of air,
seeing daylight fade into night.

I forgot about Nina and Shahly,
—life on our mountain was over too soon:
downward we swayed with the coolies again,
then we were back on the train,
click-tak-tak through long fields,
back to Mama and home in Shanghai.

Shanghai's humid climate was the reason for a common summer ritual of airing out things that were usually kept in storage. Our family's event was staged on a stretch of lawn behind our building; old trunks were sprung open and forgotten treasures laid out on the grass or hung out in the hot sun for a few hours, only to be mothballed and put away for another year. This activity often led to some fun for everyone.

Tomboy in Silk

It rises out of the rusty trunk, from a pile of clothes
the grown-ups are hanging up to dry in the sun
—the jade-green silk dress among dusty uniforms,
once-shiny brown leather belts gone to crusty grey,
and floppy red clown pants from some old show.
Papa, the ever-ready jester, pulls on the clown red,
prances on billowing legs, a-twirl in pirouettes,
with the setter Urashka close behind in happy
furious pursuit, golden fur bristling in sunlight,
his exuberant barks scattering hot still noonday air.

But I walk off, fondling shimmering folds of silk
—my new treasure. Mama said I could have it to play.
I've seen pictures of her in that very same dress!
Mama the queen with Papa the king at her side,
both standing tall, smiling. Can I ever be so lovely?

Alone in my room, I slide myself into softness.
Silk caresses my belly, flows down, enfolds my feet.
I need to see, but the mirror hangs high on the wall.
Gathering skirt folds in my arms, I climb up on the bed.
Eyes on the mirror, I drop down the rippling cloth.
I'm the Princess Marina!
The bed now my stage, I do a small waltz step.
Soon Prince Charming takes my hand, leads me
through the ballroom to the head of the dance.

The sound of quick footsteps
outside my window snaps shut my fantasy vision.
I catch a glimpse of Ronnie and Kenny, my pals,
at a run, laughing at what they must have spied.

My fellow warriors, partners in ball games,
in scaling of fences and trees —the boys
who've accepted me into their midst,
assuring me always I'm *almost as good as a boy!*
They'll tell all the others. I sit crushed in green silk.
What will I do? How will I face them tomorrow?

Boy-Girl, A Dream

Your wish is granted, the voices proclaim.
You're a boy now, forever and ever. Enjoy.

The voices have spoken and left.
Alone in the shadows, I sit on the edge
of my dream bed, observe my new self.
Gone my long curls, and I'm wearing
a simple grey shirt, dark blue trousers.
Where's my pretty green polka-dot dress?
My dolls Vera and Ella, daughters beloved?
I guess I'm not to play with them now.
I'm not what I was—a girl who is almost
as good as a boy. I'm simply a boy.

I'm supposed to be happy. I'm not.
I'm stuck inside someone not at all me,
I want to get out, don't know how, can't.
I call out for rescue, the voices are silent.
They're gone, don't hear, won't return.

I sit on my dream bed and think:
I want back my dresses, my hair, and my dolls,

I want my old face—the girl one instead of
the new one, this boy-face I want to shake off.

•

Sunlight in the window, I stretch long on my bed.
Eyes partly opened, I lift up my arms
sink my fingers into the usual morning clump
of curly brown hair—why, after all, is it all there?
Still tangled in shadows and dream shreds

and scared about starting my life as a boy
I dare sneak a peak at my corner for toys,
and there they both sit, Vera and Ella,
in their everyday spots, just the same as before.

What if the shadows, the voices, the boy-life
were all just a dream? Maybe nothing has changed?
If that's so, I'll never again wish to be a real boy!
I sigh deep. I'm a girl—a real girl after all.

In the euphoria of early post-war years, a number of Russians living in China were caught up in the belief that the Soviet Union, having participated in the war as one of the Allies, had turned a new page and that the cruelties and abuses of Russia's own post-revolutionary period would not be repeated. The Soviet regime took full advantage of this psychological phenomenon, and launched a powerful repatriation drive among émigré communities both in the Far East and in Western Europe. In Shanghai, a large proportion of the Russian community (about a quarter of the total according to some sources) decided to accept Soviet citizenship and return to the "homeland." Others were not so trusting, and the community itself began to divide along political lines. Friends, and sometimes family members, prepared to separate, probably never to see each other again. The atmosphere was tense and, inevitably, the mood penetrated into my childhood world.

Stalin and Other Stories on the Roof

We're allowed on the roof garden now
and it's fun to play there. Sometimes planes
fly really low and we can see them close up—
the letters USA mean they're from America.
One day, Shurik told me he saw a plane
so close he could see the pilot's face.
I wish I'd seen that. He's so lucky!

The roof is a good place to read too.
Mostly we read comics about the Marvels,
but one time Shurik's Mama came up
and brought along a book about Stalin.
She read aloud as we sat looking for planes.
Stalin's the leader of Russia, we learned.

He's a hero now, but the book also told
about him as a boy, when he dreamed
he could make people's lives better one day.
Later Shurik and I talked about Stalin,
we decided we want to be heroes like him.

Now when we make promises,
we say, *I give my Stalin word of honor.*
That's our strongest oath.
When Mama heard me say that,
she smiled that little smile
— it means she doesn't like what I'm saying
but she won't say why. Smiling gently,
she suggested a different oath,
like *I give my noble word of honor.*
I want to please Mama, and I try,
but saying *noble word of honor* feels funny
when I'm with my friends.
I wonder what's wrong with a Stalin word of honor.

On My Godfather's Lap

As he sat me down on his lap,
saying this was our last time together
he placed a silver bracelet on my wrist
— a token, he told me, not just of him
but the life we had shared in Shanghai.
Admiring the delicate charms on my wrist,

I couldn't think what to say, couldn't grasp
Uncle Tosia was saying his final goodbye.

A picture I'd seen a few days before
in a newspaper left on the table
came back to me then: boys and girls,
lots of them, were standing on deck
of a ship waving white hankies.
I remembered asking Mama about it
as we walked together somewhere.
She tried to explain:

In the big war that's finally over,
Russia helped the good countries to win,
so some people believe that Russia has changed.
They want to go there and help it rebuild.
Russia is inviting people like us to return
to our homeland, especially children.
Some parents are sending their children ahead
so they can study in real Russian schools.
In the picture, the boys and girls are waving
goodbye to their parents and friends.

Still walking along, Mama turned,
would you like to go, she asked with a smile,
and an icy chill rippled deep down my spine.
Would they send me away all alone?
Was she teasing, or saying they might?
I said *no!* She could see I was scared.
Not another word was said about that.

I sat on my godfather's lap and fingered
the intricate trinkets of silver, miniature
versions of objects I'd known all my life
—a bowl with two chopsticks, a basket
for chickens, a monk's drum and stick,
an abacus strung with the tiniest beads,
a wondrously layered pagoda.

Holding me close on his lap,
Uncle Tosia explained he was going
to Russia because his mother and sister
decided to go, and he did not want them
to be all alone without him. He didn't say
he wanted to stay, but I think he did.
We sat quiet some moments, I felt
a soft kiss on my hair—he was gone.

Tension among Russian families was growing not only because of the
repatriation drive. China's civil war, which had been more or less on hold
during the World War, including China's war with Japan, had resumed in full

fury as early as 1946. For us, the future was full of uncertainties. Yet, at first, the hostilities were far away from Shanghai, and we, the children, carried on our routine and untroubled lives a little while longer.

Schooldays resumed at the end of the summer of 1948, which had included my recovery from meningitis and time spent in the mountains with my father. It was my second year at the Convent of the Sacred Heart, and by this time, I was feeling the influence of a Catholic education. That, as far as my mother was concerned, fit in well with her Russian Orthodox parenting.

The Sacred Heart

Mother Robaire gave me a picture of Jesus
and his sacred heart, and I keep it near my bed.
The heart has a crown of thorns around it,
flames rise from it, a cross burns in the flames.
It means that Jesus loves us and suffered for us.
Mama doesn't mind that I love this picture
—*We believe in Jesus too,* she reminds me.

The nuns and the girls at school adore the Virgin Mary
because she's lovely pure and kind. I adore her too.
I visit her statue in the school chapel in the morning,
and I always bring one carnation—white or soft pink.
I pick it out with Mama at the market on the way to school.
I place my carnation in a vase near the Virgin Mary
then I get down on my knees and pray to be like her.

Sometimes Mother Robaire talks about the poor:
Poor people represent Jesus on earth
—when we give to them, we give to Jesus,
but we can only give to Jesus if our conscience is clear.

We learn this lesson in the month before Christmas.
Each morning that month, a poor Chinese girl sits
by a tree in the school garden. She holds an empty sack.
We girls line up, each with a potato in our hand.
If we feel pure, we put our potato in the poor girl's sack.
If we know we have sinned, we keep the potato.
Every day I bring my potato to school from home.
I want to be honest, but one day I remember a sin I did,

like maybe I was mean to another girl. So I keep my potato
while the poor girl looks sadly but kindly at me. I feel shame
but I also feel proud and purified because I've been honest.

Honesty is hard.
I learn that lesson when we make the sign of the cross.
Mama says I should do it the Orthodox way, even at school.
The nuns and other girls keep their hands open
and cross themselves from left to right.
I'm supposed to keep three fingers together
and cross myself from right to left.
I'm embarrassed, so I do it like everyone else.
I tell Mama the nun told me to do that,
and she decides she will go speak with the nun.
I cry, I confess I made that up, about the nun
—the nun never told me how to do the cross sign.

Mama is teaching me that lying is a great sin,
and lying about a nun was my greatest sin.
Now when Mama talks to me about sin and lying,
she reminds me of my *Sin about the Nun*.

I'm scared because I sin a lot.
Sinners go to hell when they die.
It's horrible, dark—hot flames, everything hurts, burns,
everyone's screaming, yelling. It never stops.

I want to go to heaven where there's light
and clouds and music and God and angels,
but you have to be without sin to go there.
I never lie anymore. I try to be good. I pray every night.

On the first day of school that year, I was told that I was to go to the third-grade classroom, even though I had by then completed only the first grade. Apparently I had been "skipped" as a way of compensating for the year I had lost while being tutored in French for the French school I ended up never attending. I had been older than my first-grade classmates, and now I was to join my age group. My third-grade experience was not entirely a happy one.

Arithmetic Class

Mother Frances is tall and thin and scary,
she's very strict, her face is always serious.
She's the first teacher we see every morning
and she teaches the hardest class—arithmetic.

For homework we have to memorize
a new multiplication table every night.
At the beginning of each class, we all stand
behind our chairs while the Mother says
multiplication questions. If she says *three times three*,
the girl she points to has to say *nine*, very fast.
If she doesn't speak or gives the wrong answer
she has to sit down—
she won't get any more questions that morning.
The first ones who sit down are in disgrace.
I'm almost always in disgrace.

Mama says I have to memorize really hard,
so hard that if someone wakes me from a deep sleep
and asks *what's four times five*, I'll shout out *twenty*
without even thinking about it.
I memorize and memorize.
Mama might test me by waking me up some night.
She doesn't. I still can't remember some numbers.

I think Mother Frances doesn't like me in her class.
Sometimes I'm late because we get stuck in traffic a lot.
The Mother looks angry as soon as I walk into the room.
Right away she shouts a question at me
and usually I can't answer fast.
I have to sit down and stay that way with nothing to do
while the smart girls keep standing,
proudly shouting out all the right numbers.

I'm always happy when arithmetic class is over.
No more Mother Frances—at least till tomorrow.

As time went on, American girls started to appear among my classmates. To the rest of us—mostly English and Russian girls—they seemed to be exotic creatures: They spoke English differently, their speech filled with rippling R sounds and slang words we didn't understand. They wore the same school uniforms we did, but their shoes were blocky and laced-up, different from our patent leather ones with round toes and little bows. Their hair was often cut short, in contrast to most of our braids of various lengths. And they tended to keep with each other. We treated those girls the same way we treated the few Chinese girls among us: we accepted them in our midst without knowing much about who they were, and without their knowing much about us.

Helen, on the other hand, was one of us but not quite. Her "crime" was that she was new.

New Girl in Class

Helen's last name threw us into peals of laughter we only pretended to suppress. Krasheninikov was a common-enough Russian name, no more ridiculous than many others we heard during roll call. But here was this new girl sitting in the back of the room, with big brown eyes and long braids of thick dark hair that seemed ready at any moment to spill out into a full and frizzy mess. A quiet girl who said little, in or out of class. We had no reason to dislike her or make fun of her, only that she had entered our world and disrupted something—something we couldn't even identify—and make fun of her we did. *Crash*-a-nini-kov, we'd snicker to each other as soon as the nun called out her name. I don't remember the nun's response, or whether she even noticed. Helen did. She sat just a few seats away from me, and I could tell. Though she made no response, no sign of emotion, I knew she heard. Helen and I were in the same classroom for only a couple of months. All of our lives would soon change completely, but in those two months at our school, everything stayed the same—Helen sat quietly in the back row, the nun called the roll, our clique of girls exploded in snickers and mockery.

I never saw Helen again, but decades later I learned by chance that, for several years, she had lived in a town less than a hundred miles from me. She had died in her sixties. I will never be able to tell her how much I regret my participation in that insensitive and cruel behavior of long ago.

•

American presence and influence were growing not just in the city but in our childhood outdoor life too. Comic books, chewing gum, and eskimo pie had become routine in the last couple of years. Now the boys were all playing softball—something I never learned to be good at, or like. And Herman started coming around.

Herman

Irina's family had a new friend, a young American with tattoos on his tanned and muscular arms. His name, Herman, was strange to us, not one we'd ever heard before, but maybe that was part of his mystique. Herman visited often, and Irina paraded him like a personal possession. He made his appearances on his motorbike, always arriving suddenly, often in the late-afternoon, and we would gather around him, clamoring for a ride. To re-start the motorbike Herman would jump-land his rear-end, hard, on the bike's seat a couple of times until the engine began to roar—and we stood watching, awe-struck at his agility and masculinity. Then the lucky person of the day got to sit behind him as he took a fast turn around the Garden Apartments roadways. Herman was a new kind of personality for us, and we, the children, saw him as some kind of hero. I never learned who he really was, or why he had been befriended by a family living in our complex. Was he a GI, a purveyor of black market goods? Very possibly. I was not curious about such questions, and perhaps I sensed that this was something I was not expected to ask about or know.

Our apartment included a small outdoor room, connected by a few steps to the back door of the kitchen. It was originally a servants' quarters, which our family's beloved "Boy"—alas, I knew no other name for him—occupied in the years before the war, a time of which I have no memory. In the post-war years, Boy renewed contact, coming by occasionally to say hello, sometimes staying to cook something special in the way only he could do. But his little room had by then become Papa's workshop, and as I got older, Papa invited me more and more often to spend time with him there.

In Papa's Workshop

I think Papa is happiest in his workshop,
and I like it when he invites me in to help.
He never says he wishes me to be a boy,
but I can tell he'd like a son to teach about tools.
I try to be the next best thing
    —a girl who can do boy things.

I'm learning to hammer and saw.
Papa and I work together, fixing things
and making small things to use at home.
We work together and talk, and I get to learn
about Papa's dreams, like, one day, he'd like
to be a toy maker, maybe a doll maker.

Talking about that, gave him an idea for Christmas:
We'd make Santa ornaments from papier mâché
—that's what a lot of doll parts are made of—
that would be a way for him to learn the craft.

•

Somewhere, Papa's found some tiny face molds,
nine of them, for the Santas for our tree.
But first we have to make papier mâché.
Papa has a book about that. This is new for him
and he's excited. I'm excited too because I get to help.
I watch as he starts mashing bits of paper into water,
maybe adding something else, I don't know what.
He's the master. I'm the assistant.
I tear the paper, hand him tools.

Soon he's stirred up something grey and goopy.
We pour it carefully into our molds and let it dry.
Then, look: nine tiny faces, all ready to be painted!
—the fun part for me!
I get to do the beige faces and pink cheeks.
Papa uses a fine brush for the eyes and mouths.

Mama makes the bodies—little round pillows—
and dresses them, in red and white, of course.

Child Interwoven

Their hoods hold the heads on Santas' bodies.
We glue clumps of cotton to their chins—the beards.
Oh, and Mama adds the hooks for hanging.
The Santas are ready!

When the tree is up, Papa puts the lights on first
then we hang our Santas, each on a different branch.
They're the stars of the holiday!
Everyone loves them. We smile, happy about our work.

What I didn't know at the time was that we were soon to emigrate, that for the next two years we would become nomads of sorts, people without a home or a country. Working on our Santa project, Papa was teaching himself the papier mâché technique in the hope that he would have a trade to practice in whichever country would give us a home. The closest he ever came to fulfilling his life's wish was working for a few months in a toy factory in Sydney, Australia—on a conveyer line.

As for the Santas, they somehow survived our two years of wandering the world till we finally settled in the United States. And though their cotton beards eventually took on a distinctly yellowish hue, their painted faces lost their sparkle, and their population dwindled, the last few little survivors held positions of honor at our family's Christmases for many years.

Interlude: She Goes with Me

Now, almost seven decades later, the playful and dreamy child of these memories still lives in me. She comes along everywhere, that girl whose pigtails never grew to the lush texture she'd seen in pictures of her grandmother Vera Kirill'na, the one who was a beauty once, everyone said. That girl looks furtively at her mother's flat belly wondering if a little brother or a little sister will ever come into her life, then she walks out into the small green spaces between the tall concrete buildings where she and her pals come together, where she becomes Mary Marvel, while Shurik rules the day as Captain Marvel, and Ronnie is allowed to be Captain Marvel Junior, a role he cheerfully accepts—he of the red hair and freckles and the big dopey smile, who follows us to the very edges of our world: the top of our complex's wall and its big front gate. We say *Shazam!* and the power to be all we want becomes ours. We soar into the sky, flying high, doing good deeds, rescuing men women and children from danger and disaster, amazing all who see. I cannot leave this girl behind. She's also the one who wanders out after the rain to find deep puddles in the soft ground under the acacia trees. There, in those puddles, she finds the day moon shining silver, peeking out from the murkiest, blackest water. It's so magical and lovely she can't let it go, but she doesn't know what to do with it. She goes inside, returns with paper and pencil, tries to sketch what she sees, but what comes out is just some funny-looking lines on the paper that she finally crumples up. That girl is still here, still hanging on to that moon silvering dark water. She's still wondering what to do with it.

3. Spiraling Out

As it became clear that Mao Tse-tung's forces would soon take over the country, our family was among the approximately seven thousand White Russians in China still resisting the Soviet repatriation campaign. Afraid to be left under Communist rule, they presented an appeal to the United Nations for help to be evacuated from the country. Whether or not that help would be given was by no means certain, and the mood among adults was tense.

Bezhats—A Talk With Mama

I walk away from my talk with Mama
with images flitting through my mind
—running, someone chasing, darkness,
wilderness, me running, somewhere.

Bezhats was the Russian word she used.
It means *run* or *flee* or *try to escape.*
Like *run away*— it's all the same word.

Sit down, she said, *I want to tell you something,*
and I knew this would be an important talk.
It was the same when she told me
there was no Santa Claus.
I felt a little disappointed then, but proud too
because it meant I was grown up enough
to keep that secret from the little kids.
That's what Mama explained in confidence that time.

Since then, we've had other talks
—they all begin with the same words,
sit down, I want to tell you something.

I sat and Mama sat.
She told me bad people wanted to rule China,
they were fighting, getting close to Shanghai.
Soon we might have to run, leave everything behind
except for money bags tied round our waists.
She was sewing them. She showed me one—

a little canvas pouch with straps. I fingered it,
tried to imagine putting it on and running.
Running where?

I thought about Papa's stories, how they fled
from Russia —Petersburg-Siberia-Manchuria,
by cart, by train, by boat, and maybe other ways.
They almost lost each other at a train station once
in the bustling rushing pushing crowds.
They were running away from Russia, their home.
Could something like that happen to us?

I listened quietly to Mama. I asked no questions.
I didn't know what to ask, but I went off
with images of us—Mama, Papa, and me
(I forgot about my grandmother Vera Kirill'na)
running, strapped with money bags,
bad people chasing close behind,
us running as fast as we can, always in the dark,
I couldn't imagine to where. Nowhere?

Later, sitting alone, quiet in my room,
I make a declaration to myself:
I will never smile again.

Interlude: A World in Scatters

I will never smile again, she says to herself,
and she wants them, the grown-ups,
to see, to know her unsmiling new self.

Does she understand she's angry?
Why does she have to run somewhere
from the place she's lived and played in
all her whole life?
Why can't Mama and Papa protect her?
Does she realize that in a just few weeks
her childhood life will be no more,
her playmates scattered around the world
never to see each other again
—all because people she doesn't know

want something she can't comprehend,
something that has nothing to do
with her or her life?

All will be scattered
only memory fragments will remain.

Not knowing what to do
she picks up her little camera,
Papa's birthday gift, and goes outside.
She takes pictures —
the wall where she and her pals sit
the tree they climb
the green island where they play.

She collects her comic books
—she'll give some to each of her pals,
something they can remember her by.

Late in 1948, the White Russians learned that their appeals had been successful: the UN's International Refugee Organization (IRO) would provide the Russians with transportation to the Philippine Islands and aid them in settling temporarily in a refugee camp there.

The Doll Barrel

The barrel will be the first to go—I shudder at Mama's words. She and Papa have just finished packing the old family trunk—the one that used to hold old treasures like my green silk dress—and filled it with what they call the essentials. I don't know, I don't care, what the essentials are. My eyes are on the tall steel barrel they've moved on to. It's actually an old oil barrel emptied out, cleaned out, and painted brown, so it'll work like one more trunk. They'll fill it up with things they say we can do without, like embroidered pillows, Chinese carvings, and my six dolls. That's what might get thrown into the sea tomorrow morning—my children!

Evacuation. It's a word I know now. I also know that there's disorder in the city center, that Shanghai is being taken over by the Communists, and we have to leave, fast—*bezhats,* flee.

There's a ship going out tomorrow. We get to be on it but Mama and Papa don't know how much we'll be allowed to take. Only that everything will be weighed, and some things might be thrown into the sea. Mama tries to explain that my dolls are not essential. I stand there silent, look at my toes.

I want to save my dolls! Usually, I can get whatever I want from Mama and Papa. All I have to do is beg, and if that fails, I cry. I'm good at that, my tears flow easily. But this is different. I think back to that talk Mama and I had. This is it. We're getting ready to flee. I understand without being told—there's nothing I can do.

I watch as they start to pack the barrel. There goes red-haired Nina, lying on top of a green pillow near the barrel's bottom. Nina is old, so old she was Mama's doll when she was a girl. Her eyes open and close. When I was old enough to play with her, Mama had her refurbished: she was in pretty good shape except that her skin was patchy, and she didn't have any hair. I don't know what kind of hair she used to have, but now she has real human hair—long, orangy-red. I've always loved sitting with Nina on my lap, combing and braiding her tresses, then unbraiding, recombing, and rebraiding them in a different way. She's disappeared under a second pillow, a blue one, and I may never see her again. Now Ella and Vera sit side by side on top of the blue embroidery, and a brown and yellow cushion is wedged in between them. Ella, Ellichka, named after Mama's cousin, is a refurbished doll, too. Her hair is painted on and she has a hard body, not cloth like Nina's and Vera's, so she's easy and fun to dress up. Vera is my first *new* doll—ordered from an American catalogue after the war. She's special in that way. Ella and Vera are now out of sight, followed by three smaller members of my family, and then, just before a fancy quilt covers them all up, in goes Mishka, the yellow teddy bear, wearing the blue and yellow vest I knitted with Mama's help, just for him. The brown barrel is bolted shut.

Tomorrow we board a ship called Hwa Lien. When it sails, will my doll family be on it with us? Or will it be at the bottom of the sea? This question floats through me, over and over, as I close my eyes to sleep.

As it turned out, the barrel made it onto the ship, but it wasn't sprung open again until four years later, when we finally moved into a house with space enough for its treasures. By then I was almost fourteen, and the dolls had lost their earlier importance for me.

•

Our last good-byes, boarding the ship, the beginning of the journey—my memory has retained few of those moments, so I draw on my mother's remembrance of our departure, and the weeks preceding it, as recorded in the memoir she wrote for the family late in her life:

From *From Me to You*, by Tatiana Romani, 1996

The year 1949 came around. The Chinese civil war was coming to an end. The Reds were approaching Shanghai, and we needed to flee the city. Citizens of other nations were evacuated by their governments. But the stateless Russians were in a difficult situation—who would come to their rescue? We had no country of our own. Then a rescuer appeared. It was General Douglas MacArthur himself. He was told our situation, and he understood. He was able to obtain permission from the Philippine government for thousands of Russian emigrants to settle temporarily on one of their small islands—Tubabao, to the south of the larger island of Samar, to which it is connected by a narrow isthmus. General MacArthur supplied us with U.S. Army surplus tents, field kitchens, and everything else that was essential to surviving on an island that was, in normal times, practically uninhabited. Ships for the evacuation were arranged for by the International Refugee Organization (IRO), and the Russians began leaving Shanghai.

In the late afternoon of January 13, 1949, the Hwa Lien *[the ship we were on—the first of the evacuation ships]*, had just left the harbor and was slowly moving along the Huangpu River toward the open sea. We were below deck in our cabin, settling in for the voyage. Suddenly we heard the sound of explosions outside. Not knowing what was happening, we and the other passengers rushed out on deck. This is what we saw:

Our ship was passing by the Caltex installation where Papa had worked. Approaching from shore were several company boats. One of them took a position ahead of our ship. The others lined up along the sides, and firecrackers were going off on each of them. It soon became clear that the occupants of these small boats were Papa's former subordinates at Caltex, who, in accordance with Chinese folk belief, were making noise in order to drive evil spirits out of our way. And so we proceeded along the river accompanied, for quite a while, by our "honor patrol" and the astonishing racket of exploding firecrackers clearing the way for us to our new life.

It would take us about two weeks to reach the Philippines. The SS Hwa Lien, according to information now available on the Internet, was a passenger/cargo ship built in 1907 by Denny W. & Bros, Ltd., Dumbarton [UK], which sank in a gale in 1951 off Keelung, Taiwan—almost exactly two years after it carried us from Shanghai to Tubabao. If my parents had worries about our ship's sea-worthiness, they did not express them to me. As far as I was concerned, it was the biggest ship I'd ever been on, and just being on board felt like the start of a new adventure. It turned out to be that—my memory of the journey is dominated by the storm that arose shortly after we entered upon the open sea.

On Board the SS Hwa Lien / Arrival on the Island

It rolls deep to the right and everything rolls with it.
I'm all sideways till I think I'll be upside down,
then it shifts, no stopping, just rolls the other way,
deep, all the way left, then back, all the way right,
rolling, dipping right, rolling, dipping left,
dipping deep deep, like the sea, like the storm.
I'm sick, too sick to go on deck, too sick to eat,
just want the rolling to stop. Will it stop?

We're all in a small room called a cabin—
Mama, Papa, Vera Kirill'na, and me.
Papa and I get to be in the top bunks.

I lie on my bunk right next to the porthole
watching water slosh on glass—up, down,
rippling and bubbling as the ship rolls.

After the storm calms down, I can sit up
and read a little, write a letter to Shurik.
Papa says we can send it later from Tubabao.
I'll probably never see Shurik again.
Maybe I'll get a letter from him sometime.

Morning. Sunshine. The ship is stopped.
Two dark-haired girls in a boat row in close,
they talk fast in a language I've never heard,
offer us fruit and other food and stuff to buy.
It's Manila. The main city of the Philippines.
The ship goes again, stops again. Tubabao.
Shimmer-blue sea, sandy beach, palm trees.
We wade through low waves to the shore.
Papa and other men go back and forth,
helping old people, small children, women,
carrying suitcases, boxes, all kinds of things.

Palms, grasses, vines, big leafy plants
   — a jungle, like in my book.
No houses. No streets. We will set up a camp.

The settlement of Russian refugees on the island was administered by the UN's IRO. The agency provided us with U.S. Army surplus, supplies left over from fairly recent wartime activity there by American troops. These included tents, cots, kitchen supplies, electrical equipment, even jeep parts; the refugees were largely on their own to use these resources for setting up a camp. Eventually, the IRO would establish tent offices at which immigration services from a variety of countries would process visa applications from the refugees— all of them in quest of a new home, of a country that would accept them as permanent residents.

Tubabao —Snapshots of Memory

Sandy beach washed by soft warm waves. It's hot. Palm trees
with coconuts, all hanging from the very top. A dark-skinned

boy scrambles up a palm, comes down with a large round fruit, shows us how to punch a hole for the milky juice— it cools the mouth, spills down through the chest, coolness runs all the way inside, and I drink and drink. Another day boys and girls bring mangoes to sell. Papa slices one open and I bite in. The taste is magical—a window to golden daydreams.

Green tents everywhere. A makeshift power station topped with a canvas canopy. A tanned Papa in a group of tanned men pose for a picture, all in shorts and small caps. They've built this power station, and they look happy and proud. There's a communal kitchen. Women in kerchiefs stir something in huge black pots—soup, a watery kind of borscht with floating potato pieces. Later we'll line up with smaller pots to collect this dinner to take to our tents. (I don't like it. I gulp down the soupy part first because I have to, then I mash my potatoes with a fork—they're almost OK that way.) The men have made paths, like streets. Papa nails a street sign to a palm trunk. He's named the path running by our tent *Nevsky Prospect*, after the grandest boulevard he remembers from his childhood in Petersburg.

We wear skimpy cotton clothes, the ones we have from the hottest days in Shanghai. Our little tent holds three cots, for Mama Papa and me. Vera Kirill'na is next door in her own tent. We have a chair. Papa made it out of a jeep seat. People who got here after us have to share large tents. Families separate themselves from other families by hanging up sheets. Sometimes those tents explode in sounds of shouting, crying, screaming. *Another tent squabble,* Mama says. I'm not supposed to pay attention.

I make friends with Irka, from a few tents away. She has flaming red hair done in thick long braids. I wish I had hair like that! We have some bubble gum from an older girl, and we blow bubbles, then have fun stretching out the goopy pink ribbons—out, and out, and . . . Oh, no! It's all tangled up in Irka's beautiful hair! Nobody knows how to get it out. Irka's grandmother, looking grim, takes big scissors and chops off her braids, right at the base. Irka's being brave about it, but she looks like a different girl, short red hair sticking out all around her head.

Swimming is every day. We walk into the water wearing sneakers to protect our feet from the sharp coral—it's everywhere, even close to shore. But shoes aren't enough to protect me from the stingray. I feel its sharp stab in my toe, which grows big and red and hot. I have to lie on my cot for days, till the poison is gone.

At night there are campfires and we sing songs. One time, the grown-ups stage a play. Mama plays the main part. She looks pretty, and she's funny. Later, the Americans bring in movies and show them on a big screen they've set up. We kids sneak in from the back, watch a movie called Robin Hood.

An excursion with the grown-ups—to the stone quarry. What for? To build something in the camp? I don't remember. Another excursion—around the island, just to explore. But we can't go all the way around. The island turns out to be a peninsula, connected by a small isthmus to Samar, the big island. Along the way, a man named Yura climbs up a palm tree, just like the Filipino boys, to get a coconut, but halfway up he's attacked by giant red ants. He scrambles down *fast*, but the ants have to be pulled out of his skin, one by one—it takes a long time. When that's over, we go on. At the end of the day, I dance on the beach with the grown-ups, all of us draped in garlands of seaweed.

People are talking about typhoons. They bring giant swirling winds and rains. We could be blown away together with our tents. Scary.

School in a big tent. A man with an American accent spreads a map on the ground and we squat around it. He points to parts of the map and says the names of American states. We repeat what he says. They're just words. I start having a sore throat a lot and Mama says I'm too sick to go to school. I don't mind.

Everyone worries about typhoons. They're coming. Everyone wants to leave but they have to wait for some country to take them in, to give them a visa. Then they have to wait for transportation. Everyone is waiting. We're waiting. Papa goes every day to find out about getting a visa to somewhere. It's just like he used to go to work. Every time he comes back, we ask, *Are we leaving?* He shakes his head. We can't go to America just now. One day he says we might go to Venezuela. Another day it's Paraguay. We might have to learn Spanish. Then the big day: Papa comes back from the big immigration tent with news. *We're leaving! We're going to Australia—we go in three days!*

Sitting on a plane, the first time ever. Air pockets—Mama has warned me. The plane feels like it's dropping, dropping. I hold my breath: *air pocket,* I say to myself. I hear a scream somewhere behind me. Someone doesn't know about air pockets, I guess. The dropping stops and everything goes quiet. The plane keeps flying.

Darwin, Australia. The airport is a big field, and we spend the night in a building nearby. Nothing else around. In the morning I see an Aborigine girl sitting in the dirt playing with a boomerang. Then we're back on the plane. I think about the girl with the boomerang. She becomes a picture I keep, like a dream. We fly on to Sydney. A new life will begin soon, but it won't last long. The girl with the boomerang will linger.

Our family spent a year and a half in Sydney before receiving U.S. resident visas, which some of our relatives, already settled in California, helped us obtain. My mother still had her mink coat from our Shanghai life; she sold it to pay for our passage on a ship called the SS Aorangi, which carried us across the Pacific Ocean—with overnight stops in Fiji and New Zealand— to Vancouver, Canada. From there we traveled to the U.S. by train, arriving in San Francisco in late April 1951. I was eleven years old. I draw again from my mother's memoir:

From *From Me to You,* by Tatiana Romani, 1996

The *Aorangi* took us as far as Canada. Our immigration papers were processed in Victoria, where American officials boarded our ship for that purpose. We then sailed on to Vancouver, the ship's final destination, where we had a day to spend before continuing our travels. It rained that whole day, so we gave up on sightseeing and went to the movies. By evening we were on a train bound for California. Our official port of entry into the U.S. was Blain, Washington, which we didn't even see, since we passed through it in the dark of night, not even stopping.

The train trip along the West Coast of the U.S., through Washington and Oregon, in April, when the mountains are still covered with snow, took us through landscapes of incredible natural beauty. We couldn't stop gazing at the wonder of it all.

In Oakland, California, we were met by my Uncle Vitia and Aunt Pausia and by Lidochka and Kolia Hrapoff, old friends from Shanghai. From there we crossed the bay into San Francisco by ferry, arriving on April 29, 1951. The very first roof over our heads in America was that of the Russian Orthodox Cathedral, the old Skorbiashchenskii Sobor. As it happened, we arrived there at eleven thirty in the evening. It was Easter night, and the Easter midnight service, the *zautrenia*, was just beginning.

4. Reviewing the Weave

To My Mother

You're everywhere in these pages.
I didn't understand then,
when it mattered to you,
the strength of your influence
or the depth of your love.
Often you wished I was more like you,
in the end you seemed to think
you'd failed as a mother. Did you?
Why do I still fear your disapproval?
Why do I still try to please you?
And why do I still make mind notes
of things I should tell you,
some small story or thought
you might like the next time I call,
until I remember — I can't?

To My Father

Long before I started really to write
I sent you some doggerel verses
describing our everyday family life.
You teared up, sensing your talent in me.
You were a presence, a true father-friend.
When absences had to be, as they do,
you wrote poems to about and for me.
Even now, now and then,
your shadow seems near, passing by,
looking in, expressing concern.
I've written some poems here
to about and for you.
I'd like to think they would please you.

Always with the Sea

With my child's eyes, I first saw you yellow
—the war was over, everything changed,
and we took our first excursion out to the sea,
a yellow sea, rippled sand, warm waves,
yellow water, three feet deep going on and on
as far as you could walk, as far as you could see,
and Mama couldn't get me out of there.

Leaving China
on the Hwa Lien along yellow waters,
the Huangpu, then the wider Yangtse,
then out to the open sea, the Yellow Sea
      —yellow, yellow, yellow.
And the next time I looked
it was all the blues in the world.

Standing on deck
how could I know I'd left childhood behind?
I was entranced by the dance of the waves,
even the greys in the virulent tossing of storm
till up to an island we rolled on the back of a wave,
a roving, crystalline blue, swishing, washing the sand.

Later
Sydney's wide beaches, its harbor of grace,
and then I stood on a ship's deck again
traversing the ocean Pacific
crossing hemispheres
voyaging north and northwest.

Hour after hour
I stood on the deck of Aorangi,
eyes on the curve where sky touches sea
then on near waves
watching them lap against the ship's side,
blue froth to white, the foam shining, folding,
breaking below, humming and hushing,
coming and going, receding, returning.

The Pacific—
in your depths, I found rippling playmates,
and still your songs ring in me,
your rhythms drive my heart, my blood's flow,
moving, revolving, resolving
the motions and moods of my life.

•

Looking Back

Lamplight falls on my hand
gnarled and scarred by the years
as my fingers linger over a keyboard
in search of words that will capture
the shadows voices sensations
arising still from the whirlpool
that churns in the bone of my skull.

My hand warm in my mother's
my father's voice, deep vibration of calm.
My face in a mirror— is that what I look like?
—blue eyes with gold-speckles
curly hair twisted to braids.
Sitting warm in the bath
my body skinny and smooth
skin stretched over ribs
legs that can run jump and climb.

My playmates' bright laughter—
their calls ring amid buildings of stone
and green grassy islands
and there, on the tree by our wall.

Summer heat and zinging cicadas
moonshine in puddles
night whispers of grown-ups
fear in the dark of something that lurks.

Blackouts, bombings, dark city—
soldiers bikes rikshas and trams.

Swaddled baby alone on a sidewalk.
The streets glisten with rain.

Legless beggars display open wounds
hold out hollow hands while we uniformed girls
sit at our desks and watch black-clad nuns
chalk small words on a shining black board.

Cross-topped domes loom above airy pagodas
narrow alleys teem with vendors, food carts,
bustling crowds, and the clamor of voices mingles
with car horns that pulse through boulevards.

War's end— the dragon prances with joy
flower-filled arches spring up on large junctions
colors of neon illumine tall buildings at night.
Soldiers and sailors stand on ships' decks
gazing out to the port, and we have our first tastes
of bubble gum pink, the chill thrill of eskimo pie.

Civil war brings back darkness—
the last crack in my childhood.
I abandon my playthings
leave them for friends to remember me by.
There I stand, on a ship's deck
watching our city fade far
then completely away.

The moments stream on
one whirls into another
past into present, tomorrow from today
child swirls into girl into woman
who twines with the child
and I, now old woman
arrange remnant moments
save what I can to my page.

AFTERWORD

The Next Sixty-Five Years

During our one and a half years in Sydney, Australia, I turned eleven, got a taste of the English school system, and acquired what was considered good penmanship. I made friends with a chubby redhead named Joan who lived next door and went to the same school I did. Joan and I corresponded for some years after I left the country but drifted apart by early adulthood. From Sydney, I also carried out an Australian accent and a pair of pretty patent-leather shoes, both of which marked me as an outsider in my first American school. I spent my adolescent years in California trying to make believe I had easily slipped into the life of a typical American teenager of the 1950s. But I never was that. I didn't manage to become "popular" in high school, even though I joined a variety of clubs, especially in my freshman and sophomore years. Eventually I settled into a stable group of friends who were eccentrics of various sorts—two of them, Olga and Xenia, also daughters of Russian émigrés, have remained my lifelong friends. The three of us found our social life in San Francisco's organizations of Russian émigré youth—and it was there, in a Russian coed scouting group, that I met my first husband, Sasha.

He is the father of my children, Elena and Alex. By the time we were married, Sasha was an officer in the U.S. Army, and his career took our family to many parts of the U.S. as well as to Thailand, where we spent two years during the height of the Viet Nam war. Sasha and I married young and struggled together through the early lessons of living as adults. We shared good times, but our seventeen-year marriage did not survive military life and growing differences between us. We were divorced in the mid-1970s, when I felt moved to join the sixties' generation, succeeding only partially because of my responsibilities as a single parent of two teenagers. I was briefly married a second time, to a Russian I met in the then Soviet Union.

During and between marriages and other adventures, I completed a Master's degree and taught English, Russian, and translation at the college level for about ten years; then I became an editor, eventually managing a publications program at a UCLA humanities research center, in a career that lasted over twenty years. After retiring, I began working on a family memoir and rapidly found myself spinning out of prose into the freer but tighter medium of poetry. The present collection grew out of those beginnings. While I was in the last stages of assembling it, I unexpectedly renewed contact with my childhood friend Shurik, after a lapse of some sixty-five years. That story is very new and may want telling one day.

My parents were relieved and grateful finally to have a permanent home in the United States. After an initial adjustment period, both became teachers of Russian at the Defense Language Institute in Monterey, California, where I finished growing up, if that's ever possible to do. Mama became active in the local Russian Orthodox Church. Papa helped out, especially with any needed craftwork. He never stopped enjoying craftsmanship and, once retired, he would putter for hours in his garage-workshop and, when occasion allowed, enjoyed teaching his grandson some of his skills. He flew the American flag on all national holidays. Papa died in 1976, at the age of seventy. Mama continued to work tirelessly on church projects and related charities well into her old age and declining health. She died in 2004, at the age of eighty-five.

I now live in Monterey, California, not far from my son, Alex, and his family. My daughter, Elena, lives in New York City, and we manage to meet with some regularity. I'm the proud grandmother of four interesting and smart young people, to whom I am Babbi. My small, if scattered, family is the essence of who I am. I feel enriched by excellent friendships—some recently acquired, some spanning most of our lives. And I take pleasure in the solitude I now claim as my own, which allows me to indulge in long oceanside walks, and writing, often late into the listening silence of the night.

Monterey, California, 2016

www.ingramcontent.com/pod-product-compliance
Lightning Source LLC
Chambersburg PA
CBHW071408040426
42444CB00009B/2146